AF284635

j. t. baka

everysome.pad sounds

one mini-album of lyrics

may day

staring out the window

staring at the rain

staring at a scene

from a hiroshige print

in my hand

my smartphone

messaging women

I met

on a dating site

messaging back

and forth

while staring

at the rain

impatiently

the one

I really like

the one

I really want

is taking her time

while the rain

is blackening

the scene

in front of me

a view of my soul

at night

on a rainy day

happyones

I

someone

somebody

everyone

everybody

someone for

somebody

some

one

for

some

body

everyone for

everybody

every

one

for

every

body

someone for

everyone

some

one

for

every

one

somebody for

everybody

some

body

for

every

body

someone for

everybody

some

one

for

every

body

somebody for

everyone

some

body

for

every

one

<u>II</u>

I am

someone

I am

somebody

I could be

everyone

I could be

everybody

you are

someone

you are

somebody

you could be

everyone

you could be

everybody

someone for

everybody

somebody for

everyone

I

for you

you for

me

it could be

everybody

happybody

DOWN

I am

who I was

I wasn't

my parents

I am

who I was

I wasn't

my school

I am

who I was

I wasn't

my university

I am

who I was

I wasn't

my love

I am

who I was

I wasn't

her death

this pain

isn't me

I was

who I am

this country

I am not

I was

who I am

this city

I am not

I was

who I am

this job

I am not

I was

who I am

this person in the mirror

I am not

I was

who I am

this body

I am not

I was

who I am

this wound

I am not

I was

who I am

this blood on these hands

I am not

I was

who I am

this knife in these hands

I am not

I was

who I am

this life

I am not

my pain

wasn't me

it just

was

UPSIDE

UP

tampon blitz.l'art pour l'art

a thought of farts

a fart of sorts

sorts of

the sound of heaven

coloured my eyes

I like

to take

pictures of clouds

I like

to take

pictures of flowers

does this

make me romantic kitsch

the sound of love

photoshopped my taste buds

I'd like

to take

pictures of boobs

I'd like

to take

pictures of pussies

does this

make me perverted filth

what if

I am

a romantic pervert

full of kitschy filth

I should

take

pictures

of skinned cats

and faded blossoms

bathed in blood

of aborted children

or even cuter

bathed in blood

of slaughtered baby seals

just to break on through

to the safe side

of art

a new knife

is like a new life

or a new wife

for cutting the cake of the maid

don't be late

BLOOD artsybloodyfartsyartsybloodyfartsyartsybloo
dyfartsyartsybloodyfartsyartsybloodyfartsyartsyblood
yfartsy BLOOD artsyfartsyfartartartfart BLOO
D fanybloodyfancyfancy B L O O D fartartartfa

NSuCKOR

lullaby

lullaby

lullaby

baby don't cry

lullaby

lullaby

baby don't lie

lullaby

lullaby

baby go die

lullaby

lullaby

baby good bye

lullaby

lullaby

baby don't cry

lullaby

lullaby

baby don't lie

lullaby

lullaby

die die die

lullaby

lullaby

bye bye bye

lullaby

lullaby

lie cry die

bye

arrested development

indeed

people die

and vampires

don't

Credits

Starting point (first idea): 903, 27th of March 2021.

Written (analogue): 903, from the 29th of March 2021 until the 18th of July 2021.

Written (digital): 903 & 925, from the 2nd of April 2021 until the 19th of July 2021.

Writer: j. t. baka.

Photographs: Simon Wagenschütz.

This is the O.L.T. to the book *Endlich. Erinnerungen* by Otaru Tomis which contains *DOWN* and *arrested development*. *Endlich. Erinnerungen* was published by BoD in August 2021.

Impressum

Redaktionsschluss: 12.08.2021.

©2021 baka, j. t.
Herstellung und Verlag: BoD - Books on Demand,
Norderstedt.

ISBN-13: 9783754328521.

Thanks to

Judit & Frank

Hildegard

Silke

Bärbel

Anne

Lydia, Martin & Anja

Christine

Adnan

Kazuko

Fred

Dr. Joachim Wittkowski

Prof. Dr. Heinz H. Menge

Yoko Tsuno

Jethro Tull

FSC
www.fsc.org
MIX
Papier aus ver-
antwortungsvollen
Quellen
Paper from
responsible sources
FSC® C105338